Heart's Apothecary

~Chapter of Enchanting Love~

Beautiful Spirit

Oh how I long for you
The nearing of your heart is as the sun on my skin
I feel your breath, your eyes watching me too
Indescribable you are, I know I am akin.
With my heart to yours
Blood and tears steady at the brim
Bared open and revealing battlescars,
How do you still love me?
Indestructible, irresistible, unconditional
You silently listen to my plea
It's happened before, it's almost traditional.
I hate that I hurt you
But I ignore your warnings and subject myself to the pain,
The only hurt I've subjected you to
Is breaking your heart, you're in full view
Watching my heart break and weaken, the impure love they gave me-
it only made me strain.
How I love you, never wanting to disappoint
I wish to please you, and make you proud
I felt your love when you did anoint
My head overtook my heart and grew too loud.
I was warned that the heart is folly
Everything in it is fake,
But you belong in my heart, happy and not melancholy.

Eyes of a Lover

I've seen you, your eyes at least.
The beautiful melody I heard when I saw them never did cease.
Eyes that see me and not look through
Come close, don't just stare from across the room.
I beg you not stay a display in my mind
Leave a map so your position I may find.
A heart as pure as snow and your will as strong as ice.
You're determined, as am I, but will we make the wrong sacrifice?
Sunlight blended turns your iris green
Thoughts flicker their shade but it's meaning unseen.
Pupils dilate at every sight
Eyes turn royal blue come the night.
Stifled might the night try
Your eyes countlessly reflect the starry sky.
Brightness comes with joy
Although all this is viewed, they have their own voice.
Oceans roar and waves bellow
Astute sculpture couldn't be accomplished by Donatello.
I know you not, we've not even met,
But I can't not love you, I've become entangled in your net.

Trust

They say beauty comes in all forms,
Yours happens to be a strong leading force
I watch as you strike and break through the storms
Show no weakness, I can't afford it of course.
I'm a leader every minute, every day
No time to waste, nowhere to stay.
Is it wrong to want someone else to take charge?
How can I trust you? I can't just let down my guard.
A power struggle at best, a display of leadership in battle
You don't care for looks and strength, no war or shackles.
A gentle whisper is what you crave, not a disparage,
You don't have to earn it, just take the reins- ask my hand in marriage.
Feats of strength and power surge
Time and time again victorious you emerge.
Like thunder pangs your persistence roars
Lightning strikes and you fight the wars.
Year after year you captain the ship
Even emotionally you could lift the titanic.
Heave and throw
When nobody watches you still continue, it's not for show.
I never thought I'd meet my match
Someone exceeds my talents
In comparison mine doesn't even make a scratch
The weight of the world on your shoulders yet you remain gallant.

My Heartbeat

Pay attention, my love, to the beat of my heart.
The small but ever so fragile organ,
The one so many tried to rip apart.
I couldn't think of sharing it, not even in portions.
That's since changed.
In your hands, my heart rests entirely
The eerie sadness and heart pangs!
Held it gently and calmed it's storm, now beating quietly.
By the oath of my bleeding heart,
I swear to love you longer than the stars
To do what you wish and crave
For being so able, my heart you did save.
At your service and in your command
I stand proudly by your side
Knowing in my every best interest you refuse to demand
With you my heart has no lack of an unconditional guide.
It's all for you: the seemingly effortless breaths, the oxygen traveling
through my veins.
Can you hear it? The gentle murmur it speaks.
Taking away toxicity and pain.
That second, every second is for you. For you- oh how it beats!

Test by the Tempest

A trial, a trial- "By fire," they say!
Thrown into the deep end and a storm arises.
Keep breathing, try to stay above the fray.
If you are able, stay alive until the sun rises.
Yet when does that dawn so break?
Through counted gasps and waves hit
A fear that the sun itself will be late
Charcoal grey clouds cover the sky, there's no blue, not one bit.
A ship recklessly crashing through the waves,
Use your muscles, paddle a smidge
The wood looks ragged coming towards you, cautious now, or it'll
send you to the grave.
Perhaps you can move out of the way before you're dashed to bits.
A miss! Not by far, pushed to the side!
No, wait! Is that a bar? A rung at that!
Hurry now, the storm has just begun to screech, wail, and cry.
Conn the ship as you please, but the wind and waves formed a coup
d'état.
Black forms grow larger and more jagged with every knot,
Steer against the waves, not with!
Rain and seawater sting your eyes, but keep them open, you ought!
Do you want to capsize and be labeled a myth?
It's no use! The wind and waves steam on,
An empty ship has no chance to persist.
To these craggy rocks this ship is drawn

A shipwreck! A crash, saltwater, and nothing more than mist.
Holding the buoy while balancing your tired body feels nothing more,
Scanning for large enough driftwood to leap to.
The hardened heart and softened wood paddle on, not sure which way
to shore.
How easy that would be, alas! Should the storm not exist and cease to.
Navigating through the wooden battered remains,
A spot of darkness in the distance.
Could it be? Land at last! Oh those far but beautiful plains.
Tired body screams, but there's no way around stubborn persistence.

A smaller wood to shift and steer.
Closer and farther you go, being thrashed by waves to and fro.
Battling the current! In your hand not a plank, but a spear.
Is it but an island? It is not! Sweet mainland, how you glow!
Take hold of the dock now, and let go not one bit
Should a tidal wave come, and force you to quit.
The wind is screaming and the rain- stops.
Look up, there it is! Blue, and yellow! The beautiful sun and sky
appear in spots.
Oh what beauty does the dawn break!
What tired body does so ache,
Soaked and shivering, joyous in all,
It's over now, there is no more nightfall.

Surefire Heart

Beauty beyond imagination is what you are.
These things you do, they are not even close to subpar
Your duties all fulfilled, everything perfect on your listed devoir.
What sweetness to my teeth to make me tremble,
A gentleman at that and well suited for sure.
Nothing can come close, nobody can reach or resemble.
There's none, not one illness you cannot cure.
The breath of your lips raises my skin,
My jaw clenches when I say your name.
My eyes close and a smile flashes as I wait for the lead-in,
Your hand in mine and I see clearly a little lantern with a flame.

A Mandrake

Those rolling hills, the green cliffside surrounding
Grass wisps around, the wind passes by unresounding.
The only light is the rays of day,
Think about it as you stroll through the mandrakes.
Look up from those purple flowers divine
Up to the sky and ponder, "When will those stars align?"
A pocket filled with mayapples that aren't for you,
Things will turn out, maybe. If only you knew.

Save Me

How great was your love
That you could help me believe thereof!
I couldn't help my heart, but you could
I felt warmth and all that's good.
The peace you bring I can't
Replace it with anything, no I shan't.
To love you is to give everything a rest
I'm struggling to see how I'll pass this test!
It's all from you I admit
I'm trying to conduct myself to well acquit,
And tear down these walls I built
Everything right down to the hilt.
Stay with me until I fall asleep,
Just hold me for a bit, I'm yours to keep.

Music Box Heart

I refer to it as my music box heart:
Fragile, complicated, and tedious.
It's frustrating, you know, when you're missing a part.
It plays the same song, unaware of anything previous.
You don't have to like it, no need for it to be destroyed.
It's not easy to put together, but worth it in every way.
Open it, you're tempted, but your eyes can't avoid
A shiny nick-nack ticking away at chords, be careful, it's not just a
display.
Do everything perfectly, and don't miss a beat,
I can't, I mustn't stop! Until the end of time.
Wind up, play, repeat.
The one who stays to listen- that love will be mine.

Compass to Your Heart

Seeking you, I'm lost in the crowd
Your voice is loud
I'm in darkness, but you're all I need.
Surrounded, but you're all I see.
I'm trapped in the fray
I call out now and then.
My heart has weight
But I then I remember when,
My tears go dry
I need to let you in.
Your love is like an heirloom
Precious heart's tune of mine,
Beauty never gone to soon
Yours until the end of time.
You say the heart is tender
And people are my downfall,
So you can guard it forever
With it under key and lock.

Prince Charming

What a beautiful number it is, twenty-two:
The day beautiful people are born on, the first day of life, and a day of
freedom for three.
The first time a man's love came through,
I was in tears and got swept off of my feet.
It felt fitting for this to be about you,
I know your intentions were only true.
When beauty fell from great height
And suffered not one but two great frights,
Prince Charming ran through dust wind and rain,
Saved the girl and kissed better the pain.
Limp in your arms she lay with tears strolling down.
Slaying those dragons and walking that same path you took,
Calming her wails and taking care not to break her crown.
Hiding her in love unconditional, tucked away in safety's nook.
You live through beauty in grace,
Even though not here, she'll always remember your face.

Perfectionist in the Pages

Open the book
A clean slate.
Hero or villain? They're all starting to look.
What do I say?
Out into the arena
Everyone sees
I'm out in the open
And they're all bigger than me,
but I have the grace of a ballerina.
Do what they expect, the unspoken.
Don't falter. Don't break,
Do everything with purpose,
You're up! Don't bend. Don't quake.
Behave or they'll see your inner circus.
Turn the page,
Oh, a fresh start!
Is it? Or is that you offstage?
Nobody sees your mind is tart.
Jaded, I need to be perfect.
I can do better.
Do you? You're gold-flecked.
You are enough, you aren't a debtor.
Valid, that's you.
Your perfection is your best
Take your time, see how it's true.

Don't listen to them, take a rest.

15

Circumference of a Covenant

The circumference of a gold ring, a promise
Glowing it surrounds me,
Everything you say, I know it's honest.
To the cliffs and dark areas I see the dark ones flee.
The black mist of the evil rises
The confusion it brings doesn't cloud your light
They plot and scheme all of good's demises
Try as they might, and we know they will, it will end with their blight.
Perceive internally, there is no grey divide
Choose your eternity and live it well,
It's only final when you decide,
To end the curse and break the spell.
Stay in your glowing ring of covenant
Do the right thing, even if not relevant.

Battle Storm

From dark skies to barren fields the wind sweeps
And the swaying willows weep,
The portals above know
The chariots roar from door to door.
Prepare for battle, lightning strikes
Clouds swirl and pool together
The mighty flag of agriculture raises at first light.
It's only routine, you understand, like clockwork is forever.
Sparks fly when metal clangs
Electric lights and loud thunder pangs.
You went to far, you missed your chance
Go back, there's still room perchance.
Dawn til dusk the sky is tilled
'Til no more rain be milled,
The drought above floods the earth
Understandable when the sun is the hearth.
Plants liven and soil turns black.
Hurry, the door is closing
There is no going back.
Let him go, he's not opposing.
The horses gallop and the soldiers gallant,
The metals blaze across the sky
The sun attempts a burst through the clouds but isn't valiant.
All this just to reach the other side.
Bodies unscathed and rigid no more,

The work is done, the storm is over.
For unclenched jaws and sheathed swords
Let rest be the soft reward until next changeover.

Work of the Wind

The willowy wind waves to and fro
Rain or shine it persists with nothing to interrupt its flow.
Wispy leaves through the branches weave
Fly through the air and onto the topsoil beneath.
Circulate the current and grasp as it goes
Linger on chapped lips musing in prose
Sway through heels and loafers in a crowded quarter
Halt. Let the sun shine uninterrupted so the night may be shorter.
Carry on and let the grateful remember their coats
See those two? They should exchange notes.
It's neither of their fault, it's a windy day
In the fray of the papers blow every time they ask for a name.
Do a hop and a skip over the waters
Aren't you tired of those ungraceful walkers?
Make ripples and skid the pond
Nudge a little ducky closer to its mom.
Blunder through the schools and perfect the craft
Tease the people who barely feel a draft.
Excite and have fun, shoot the breeze
After all, it's the children that notice your absence who act bereaved.
A tap here a tap there
Look this way and that until there's a braid in your hair.
Which way does the wind blow?
Directly in your face as you talk to your beau.
It's all in good fun, they thought it was silly

Now you're inside with them gifting you a lily.
Be walked home and a gust goes by
It's crisp, so a jacket is lent- my oh my.
Run away, they've got it from here.
Crunching nearby, is that a deer?
I know, I know. It's a meddlesome bunch
The wind's work is never done.

Flower

Dark and cold it remains
My body desperate to stretch and stomach for food
Nutrients feel as water for my veins
So tired of others, but there must be a brood.
Dig deep and stretch my legs
Grab the water and down even the dregs
Rest and nourish as I must,
It takes time but surely I shall adjust.
Sleep and rest, to my environment I regulate
Reach and twist and turn so I must correlate.
A breath of fresh air- finally!
How cool and brisk, how I enjoy my renewed vitality!
Pull myself up from my cozy hiding place
None knew, it was my own secret formidable space.
After everything, my back and shoulders stiff
I must jive if I want nothing to be amiss.
Shake off and relax, petals curl downwards
Beautiful even by scientific standards.
Grow in bunches and groups, save for one brave
Able to hide away from the clearings, her own future she paved.

Golden Days

To sit in a field green and peaceful
The beautiful weather and nature so blissful.
Grass up to the knee but I sit anyways
In the golden hour soaking the sunshine rays.
Leaf blades as soft as silk
Brushing against skin normally pale as milk
Now golden and blue eyes green,
Lounge around and browse the unseen.
Wind swinging the leaves as fingers reaching for their maker
Peacefully untouched on a secluded acre.
Reaching or braiding? Whipping looking to inflict
Until a few were picked, such derelict.
A bush with fuzzy leaves
Like cotton it must be harvested in sheaves.
Snap a berry off the branch
Pop the sour fruit and mind the mouth-watering avalanche.
Distant tree flowers look as wool
Astounding gifts pleasant by the handful.
Grab a few and take my leave
A perfect day I'd achieved.
The sound of leaves in the wind rustling
Has a similarity to running water rushing.
Songbirds claim the minutes in harmonious tune
It all stops at night break to sleep by light of blue moon.

Future Dreams

Shooting star shoots before my eyes
I run my mind all through the night,
My screams echo but nobody hears my fright
I get lost in every future plan we devise.
Rickety, how can I keep going
When everyone else seems to be flowing?
I can't lose myself to me.
Me, me, me.
"How selfish" I think, but my every move is for you.
To work for everything you've ever dreamed, something brand new.
So beautiful this dream we plan for forever.
A wedding, a wedding!
A white dress and flowers too
My love, are you ready?
It's all on paper, take my hand and we'll go through.
"You can do it" is all I heard when I
Think I did what was right.
How could I be so wrong?
In the distance I hear you coming, your beautiful song.
And just like that,
A few words soothe my soul.
Instantaneously fast,
Your words make me whole.
I seldom forget your love, but every tune you hum
Reminds me of who we've both become.

Timeless Love

I love you in the way that wars were started for Cleopatra.
Your name has begun to ring in my mind as a mantra.
I love you in the way that makes my mouth go numb
And my thoughts fog intensely, that makes me look dumb.
I can't form a coherent thought, none bright or true
only my initial reaction remains:
"I love you".
That's all that runs through my mind:
you, endlessly. An unconditional love that seems beyond time.
I've loved you for longer than I remember,
Even cold, my heart still carried embers,
But how when both hardly even knew of the other's existence?
All it took was one glance, one momentary instance.
Before when the universe was created we were split apart
Now we just remain two halves of one heart.
How you make me stutter and stumble over my nerves
Is the same way I fall hopelessly infatuated with you by a few simple
words.

The Extract of Life

Where the love light gleams
Is where life itself is held together by the seams
Is seen in every light ray shone upon earth
As life's first breath takes flight on every infant's birth.
In every fiber of the tree bark you see
The flowers that bud in each season
Every color that surfaces in autumn, in every leaf
For each heart beat there is always a reason.
In such fear there is no small antonym
The adversary outmatches every tear shed in terror
The peace brought forth by love is to each a beautiful hymn
Everyone talks about death, but love's first love? Look in the mirror.
The kiss of Death is a one time happenstance
It's quick and clear, he's not as morbid as you assume
Love sees you and immediately thinks of romance
Every glance turns a blush into full bloom.
Love is life in every way
I hope you get this, that you receive and know it in your bones
That love keeps your blood flowing and your body warm day after day
That love itself is proud of you, watching from his throne.

A Love to Everlast

One glance into your eyes
And I'm entranced in their endless fires
They say beauty is fleeting,
But yours is recurring as the sun and horizon meeting.
The epitome of goodness and grace
A heart of gold one can only find in your embrace.
Should your life take the form of a rose, I'd keep you a well watered
flower
Each leaf carefully pruned and gardened inside,
I'd let the sun's rays in, for you it may empower
I'd sit with you and stay, to your every need I may provide.
I'll stay yours until the end of time,
And each day I know you'd be mine.
Hearing the words "to hold and to cherish"
Until the end of time I keep, past our end do we part
Long after the world's perish
In every setting and aspect my love for you I'll impart.
While this may seem forceful I must fully insist
My love for you is gentle and slow, very unlike limerence.
As innocent as a budding flower barely brushed against sweet lips,
As on a lattice, swirling vines draw observing interest.
An anticipation of the future perhaps
Where I can call you mine and I yours,
A time where we can make up for what the other lacks

And when the world crumbles around us, we know that with each
other we're secure.

27

True Love's Kiss Breaks the Curse

Fight bare and brave
Push through and make way to the cave
The beast holds it captive, a precious thing.
Can you believe it used to be the king?
Power hungry and driven mad
Corrupted by greed, my love coated ironclad.
In anticipation twigs crunch underfoot
Or at least they're twigs unless you look.
"For the good of the people" he said
But we all knew he wanted the glory for himself, what it meant.
Nobody wants to be the hero, but it must be done
I take no rest until the war is won.
Duck and avoid the cobwebs line the inner tunnels
Accompanied by stepping over armor of past soldiers, evident of their
struggles.
It's inevitable that the hands of man put the kingdom last.
Our life source, our very root
I can't blame solely the beast, part of him is the king.
It's been going on for centuries, this glorified dispute.
Lucky he was cursed in the winter with no resources, and not spring.
Cross breeze flies by whistling
Disgruntled noises indicate he can sense me near
It's almost as he's behind me, sniffling
His low rumbling I can hardly hear.
The roof grows shorter and the back wall is nigh

Growing close I feel his pride and anger growing
So intense I can't help but cry
Not sobs, but raised skin and my tears continue flowing.
Shadows shift in my surroundings,
Lantern blown out and darkness around me.
Light a match and come face to face
Escape the bewildered beast and his deathly embrace.

Bob and weave to dodge his threats
Lure him out so he may face his own regrets,
In the mouth of the cave I finally see
A king held captive by his own mind, no longer free.
Dilated pupils and hair like feathers
Body bruised and tattered, beyond weathered.
Fingernails sharpened and teeth stained red
Upon anyone else he would lay determined dread.
I know you're in there, my love, come out to play
Stop this madness, it's not a courageous display.
Lunge and attack
Just one touch, love. You'll get your kingdom back.
Keep missing me as I effortlessly dodge your strikes,
Leave claw marks in the tree where I once stood.
Your disreputable actions with one kiss a clean slate I will wipe
Awaken now, my love, reign as you should.
Backed into a corner, nowhere to go
I walk towards you unafraid, one true love's kiss.
The curse lifting releases his pride, see his original form truly show
Your mind now back from the dark abyss.
Knight nearby, take him back to the castle
Hold fast and brave the criticism
It's been years, but now it's over. All the hassle.

Return with me to your position, take care of our people, return with your heroism.

30

Borrowed Confidence

Remember the peace and joy surrounding
The nature gracing your face astounding
As sunlight through the leaves intricate patterns lay
In complex shadows and movements of display.
A beautiful triumphant sight
Rising early to share the day's first sunlight.
Unorganized and imperfect this is true,
But the day is scheduled so you can continue.
Disgruntled and filled with chaos, but it's yours to keep
The world is in your hands to break the mold, not to fall in eternal
sleep.
A rhythm emerges from each step
Bear your newfound swing of strength that society must accept.
Walking to the beat of your own drum was never impossible
You never stepped to the plate and found yourself responsible,
But now with each turn and development it's now viable
Don't give up and fall prey, you'll be unoriginal and pliable.
Keep your shoulders squared and your chin held high
You don't need borrowed confidence when you generate your own
supply.
Come, come home and join us
Remember to be humble, we have much to discuss.
Be joyous and clear
Hold your standards firm so your people have nothing to fear.
Sing as loud as you can so all may know

You act on your words, it's not all for show.
Even darkness is only the absence of light
Go forward and recall that you do what's right.

32

Starry Eyes

I've fallen for you, you see
I hope it's a start of a conversation, one that quickly makes my heart
beat.
I write you love letters, it's a wonderful way
To proclaim to you everything I have to say,
And that I fall more every single day.
Tulips are scarlet
Lavender is Calming,
Your eyes have the appearance of starlit
And it leaves the heart wanting.
They gave you that gift, a precious idea,
How befitting of those stars.
When they saw you they sang Ave Maria.
"A treasure that is only ours."
A beautiful sentiment they say
But beauty is in the eye of the beholder.
You are the epitome of grace and elegance even compared to ballet,
With a personality so fiery it continues to smolder.
They're as ever radiant galaxies.
Graceful, pretty, and beautiful.
Precisely what the stars are
Incomparable, absolutely reputable.
Dare I say, a work of art?
You're sunshine on a rainy day,
A beauty harnessed and put on display.

Inasmuch, you're my favorite season
You're as vibrant as autumn, that's my very reason.
Built like the gods of old,
Within reach but never able to grasp.
Nearly impossible, you were born with a heart of gold
Even walking leaves mortals with mouths agasp.
Mount Olympus is home to you
Golden days, powerful and strong
If only these mortals knew!
How wonderful it is, to be exactly where you belong.
In the highest regard,
For you does the morning sing!
Night altogether sees it avant-garde.
No matter, for soon does the day spring!

Vintage Kisses

Swing my leather shoes off my desk
Look out the window to the scene picturesque
Put the record player on
Sip the coffee on my desk, wonderful pecan.
Don't forget
The details of how we first met
Lean forward and type away
Type quickly on my typewriter today.
Hang off of every word Paul Anka has to say
"They floated through the night in harmony" a beautiful line to your
essay.
Pull back the platen and start the next line
Tap your feet to the music lest you be left behind.
Take out the hair pins and do a little spin
Hum along and allow love a win.
Let your victory curls fall and pick a record from them all
Choose carefully so a portrayed love may enthrall.
Lipstick stained red on glasses from nights before
Not knowing you'd be swept off your feet, what was in store.
Repeat the night, replay it in your mind
Chiseled features, everything defined.
Sway your hips and pucker your lips
"Eyes shown like an eclipse"
Oh such a beautiful chance.
Darling, do you remember the last dance?

Of you and your true lover at a masquerade ball
Safe and beloved, never letting you fall.
How he held you until the end of the night
How he swayed you like it'd be the very last time.
Every innocent kiss he stole
And every lighthearted wit, everything so droll.

Winter Solstice

Little flurries falling from the sky
Leaving breath cold and icy, a happy little high.
Nobody outside but radiating joy from houses nearby
Obviously weather is something everyone respects, nature to be
revered by.
Light and sparkling drifting through the air
All of them swift, intricate, and debonair.
So fragile and sweet
Without each snowflake no winter is truly complete.
Almost like sugar being shaken upon the earth
Before spring paving a way for foliage rebirth,
Being shaken out by God himself
Coaxing each of us together with coldness, so we feel compelled.
As if to give us a break from the darkness and war here
Each time at the end and beginning of the year,
A beautiful remedy to clear your mind
Refreshing coldness in physical form defined.
The only feeling left is to share it with loved ones
Whilst you recall your days in the sun,
To hold their hand and show them
The winter flowers you picked, holding them at the stem.
There's still peace and stillness in the fray
Enjoying each snowfall, observing each array.

Cursed by Jealousy

We thought we'd be safe here
A building veiled by trees and deer,
Abandoned ballroom late at night
Only lightning from the tempest provides the random shine.
Candles freshly blown out
Swirls of wick smoke dancing throughout.
Hide in the shadows, she can't have seen us come in.
The doors burst open, quickly she finds us within.
Our love transcends boundaries
Determined to be passed through generations, possibly centuries.
Go quick, I'll hold off the witch,
Don't make that face, I'll join you quick.
I'm determined for us to restore
As I watch you sneak out the back door,
Worried it will be your last
French doors burst open, against the thunderbolt her figure contrasts.
Jealousy walks right in.
Takes my breath away and puts an anger within.
Powerless, she gives me her awful dark brew,
Forced a dagger in my hand, and shoved me after you.
My body fights to march up the hill
She has every wicked intent to kill.
Straining muscles in a failed attempt to stop each step,
Evil creeps through my veins, making each move more in depth.
You run towards me, I try to yell.

Every ounce within me combating her spell.
I flex my arms striving to put the dagger on the ground
Nearby I see you, the physical urge to throw the blade is profound.
You're very supportive but the spell is too strong
I can't remember where this all went wrong.
Pushing it away from you with one arm and the other fighting in your direction
My heart beating louder for your protection.

I catch a glimpse of Jealousy and remember,
Seeing her from afar engulfed in her temper
Watching in the distance as we held hands
Tilting her head as if she didn't understand.
Flinching with every stolen kiss that felt like the sun
She became more and more undone,
Physically cringing when each sweet nothing was whispered in your ear.
As if she were next to us, close enough to hear.
Just like that the dagger swings, and narrowly misses might I add,
A breath of relief for your safety, a wave of peace and everything glad.
The dagger drops, and so does Jealousy to her knees
We look to each other, and silently agree.
We walk over to help but like a mist she dissipates
Our only motive was to understand, and give a clean slate.
Run inside as the atmosphere shifts,
It starts to rain and the candles inside now alit.

Lovestruck Crush

I feel like I'm losing myself to you.
I'm giving you everything and nothing is coming back.
Upon closer inspection, I'm not quite sure you have a clue.
I believe your innocence, that this isn't an attack.
You have no interest in me, I can see that clear
But I think you see this as short term,
At least that's what I fear
Leave it to one smile, that's all I needed to reaffirm.
Don't misunderstand, I love being friends
I know you do too,
At some point either my feelings or our friendship must come to an
end
I've seen your heart and know too much, I believe that's why I want to
pursue.
I don't think it can last forever.
I think you'll make a fool out of me
Irrational fears, I know, but anxiety creeps up on me whenever.
You must see it, how I feel. That my face always rises a few degrees,
That when you turn away I'm furiously writing in my diary
Or screaming in a pillow when you leave the room
Fawning over you entirely,
My emotions drowning me until they consume.
I must speak up before it's too late
But I don't have the elegance of a deer or the grace of a swan.
It's not up to me, but I've been very nice to fate

I hope it will see things the same way, I won't know how to move on.

41

Take One Chance

People never believe in the potential they should
It's time for a change, sometimes these things are good.
The things around those people, everything has to be complicated and
logical
Stop the presses, for once let yourself feel an instance so magical.
On occasion just let go
I promise it's not all bad, you won't hit A plateau.
Take a leap of faith and let someone catch you for a change
Stop planning, let another do something in exchange.
Let them hold you dear, loving you in every way
They won't abandon you, but I can't promise they'll stay.
It's scary, trust me I know
Remember, this is all for you, not some television show.
It's not a publicity stunt or a gossip team
Not everything is organized and neat
Sometimes love is messy, but not in ways we expect
Take someone's hand, give it a rest.

Lover's Absentee

A guy like him is hard to find
We all know who I'm talking about, the one that works on the first try.
He stands out, being dashing, charming, and kind
Everything that the fairytales imply.
Daydreams and musings of him run amuck
But when will he actually appear, not just in the diary of my thoughts?
Instead of pining over him, I'll be pining with him and love-struck.
I want to be very clear, let me get my point across:
Where his smile shines like the ocean reflecting the light of the moon
Someone to encourage my artistic tendencies
Who's shoulders are broad, maybe he's built like a house... or two.
With strong morals, he believes in the truth and dependency.
Who will help me decorate for the holidays
One to catch me if I fall off a ladder putting up the star
Holding me and for our relationship creating a solid base
That won't settle for anything subpar.
I have a space where he can be my hero and I can be his
A place where the heart flows until I find where he truly exists.

Physical Chemistry

I never knew a hug could leave me with weak knees
Not to mention my blushing cheeks.
But it happened. I'm shocked and surprised.
I have a feeling that hug meant the same thing for you by one look into
your eyes.
Either way it kind of surprised me,
The accuracy of this account I can't guarantee.
I've played it over in my mind a million times, maybe more
Why have I never noticed this before?
Your embrace left me gasping for air
My lungs contracting and then unmoving as if they were in disrepair,
And I couldn't get over the tingling
Each time I look into your eyes, I see them twinkling.
I've never felt that, and you gave it to me.
I lost the lock to my heart, and I think you stole the key.
In that moment I felt safe I miss that,
Now when I see you my heart undergoes combat.
That coldness of being in your arms, the briskness of your muscles
I see floating away from me all of my troubles.
The stiffness of your shoulders and chest
Lifting me off the ground without gravity's protest.
As you wrapped around me and held me so tight that I couldn't
breathe,
My entire body begged you not to let go, please.
The feeling of wanting to hold you just as tight

Has long since never left my sight.
That scent of yours that was always consistent
Floods my senses leaving my mind spinning and me reminiscent.
I miss being in your arms
Just your presence being my good luck charm.
You're so gruff and brief that I can barely catch up,
But your lips are slow to speak and perfectly plump.
Maybe you're keeping your distance
We have the same idea: avoid admittance.
Which is the right thing to do,
I'm not sure, maybe that's untrue.

Musica del Benessere

We humans have the time of our lives listening to music
Some call it joy, I call it therapeutic
To hear the call of goodness,
An extract for emotions, that's what it is.
A little happy here, a little sadness there
Helps you process life when is more than you can bear.
Leaving little marks on our hearts
Inspiring our ideas to go off the charts.
Feelings reverberating through the air
A serene feeling we can't help but share,
Like an invisible tattoo that we see as art
Sometimes sweet, but it can be a little tart.
Tradition that was placed through countless generations
Breaking through boundaries and regulations
In every culture it leaks out and inspires
Noting every event in our lives that transpires.
Holding each second captive
Reminding us that life itself is extremely attractive
Captivating our minds and enhancing memories
Removing mental illness with a natural remedy.

The Little Things

Play me like I'm your favorite
Do it, go on. I'll plead.
Every ounce of it I'll savor
I'm patient for you to proceed.
I want to see how often you listen to your CDs
When you sing along to your favorite song you're already thinking of
me,
Inspired like nobody is looking and performing like it's illegal graffiti
Singing along, but nobody knows the part of you that's a devotee.
When you say the quietest thank you when you eat your favorite food
Smiling in gratefulness that someone remembered and thought of you
Devouring every ounce of it until you conclude
No leftovers on the next day to construe.
Standing up and shouting loud
Cheering on your a-listed sports
Voice breaking as it booms above the rest of the crowd
Knowing you keep tabs on all of their reports.
Taking care of your favorite clothes
Wearing them and making necessary repairs,
Making sure no tears or seems lay exposed
So you can keep them for endless wears.
Choosing your favorite coffee
The one you pick to wake you up each morning,
Accepting it as is, even when you're grumpy and groggy
Holding the mug close because it's ever so warming.

Usually with your favorite blanket
Draped around your shoulders
Your go to breakfast looking like a banquet.
I want all of that from you, that each of us are the beauty and both of
us the beholder.

Moving Heaven and Earth

I'm waiting for you, you know.
I'm consistently driven towards the day you'll show
When you'll show up and wonder if I'm the one
I hope I'll notice you, after everything happened that fate had spun.
That you'll move heaven and earth just like I tried
But that you'll succeed, and you'll be able to make that immense divide.
Testing God to see if He made me for your very being
Nature helps as you remain focused upon foreseeing.
Rays of light break through the clouds shining only to be in my presence
My eyes dart across the field to you remaining luminescent,
Your mouth moves but I can't hear a word
Astonished, I can't believe what next occurred.
That field of flowers blossomed surrounding
I mistook a sound in the distance what I thought was my heart pounding.
It's not the correct season for blooms,
A willfully beautiful mixed aroma of the floral perfumes.
Below each of the petals crack
It must have been a million chrysalides, I couldn't keep track
Butterflies swirling tubular around me towards the sun.
Why didn't I see them and when had this begun?
Butterflies need about 3 hours for their wings to relax
I feel as if I'm in some sort of odd time lapse

Maybe they were forced out by the pounding
My eyes widen as I realize it's not my heart resounding.
Ground shaking and I see you running across the plains
Sprinting through the grass but on your pants not one green stain,
Quickly take my hands with a smile
The rumbling is getting louder but I guess we'll stay awhile.
In the distance through the woods
I see more deer rushing down the hill than there probably should
Heading right towards us but you're unmoving
I'm questioning your sanity, my face must show some disapproving.

As if we were protected in some circle unknown to man
The herd circles back around us and you reassure me the best you can.
Catching my attention, your eyes light up my world like someone
flipped a switch,
Your smile so charming and sweet, like it's used as sugar to enrich.
You have a youthful innocence to you, as if you were Peter Pan
I must be Wendy in the story, the one who always has a plan.
At the same time you have a wisdom unshakeable
Life could give you a challenge and you'd be more than capable.
The deer had gone, I'd not even noticed
I wasn't paying attention, not to them at least, but I've been focused.
The moon light breaking between us caught my attention
When I'm around you, time seems to be caught in suspension.

Gardening Hearts

Ever blooming hearts doting on the mind
Wondering where their lover is
Looking at the blueprints they designed
Giving more than they're supposed to give.
I suppose the heart is like a rose
They need gentleness to be taken care of
Beautiful yet very fragile, at least I suppose.
You have to watch for signs, I think the sneakiest is when they're in
love.
When they blossom too fast and can't weather the cold
If they get heartbroken and start to grow thorns,
You have to cover them and give them warmth to hold
Give them space and watch as they mourn.
Prune the pieces that die off
So better and healthier leaves can grow
Continue to be gentle, even when they scoff
They'll heal, the timing is just slow.
Much like roses, hearts have healing abilities
Some can help sadness and depression,
When you cut off some rosebuds, they can grow back in endless
possibilities
They're precious to the holder, but only when they're in your
possession.
That's how the heart heals, taking time and curing itself
Growing and changing as time goes on.

It's best in its own environment, not on some bookshelf
Flowers always looking for sunlight is a heart looking for comfort, take care of them or they'll be gone.
When the sun comes out you can smell the roses stronger
Like the fires of love to a heart feel like holy fire
Is like a heart when it adds more space for a new love, becoming slightly broader
Growing interest for their new addition, increasing in their desire.

It's called a heritage rose, some of them a little safe haven
I think there should be heritage hearts,
Protecting hearts from generation to generation
Shielding them endlessly from poisonous darts.
A heart sanctuary, that's what it should be
The preservationists' guide to healing hearts should come with a
manual
After being heartbroken and in pieces, I believe you'll agree
It takes a reminder and safety that hearts are valuable.

Lie Lock Silk

Lying down beside me under the silk ivory
Cerulean summer skies enticing the white lilac tree to bloom.
When you're not here every flower knows me as well as my diary
They know your story so well, every action of ours they already
presume.
Interlocking fingers, our wrists pressed together
Feeling your pulse with my own beating through my veins
The grass tracing our bodies so gently, as light as feathers
Eyes unopened but content with everything today contains.
Silky skin brushing against mine
Singular breaths moving our bodies ever so slightly
Light through the leaves shone a glossy sheen on your eyelashes
wonderfully divine
Lying interlocked softly under the lilac silk ivory.

Forbidden Love

The difference between Summer sunshine and Winter rain
Is that Winter makes you forget there ever was a Summer
And Summer takes away all of Winter's pain
Reminding you there's always room to recover.
Two opposites never to overlap
Like Spring and Autumn so similar but just out of reach
Summer insisting for Spring to speak about Winter's snow and polar
caps,
Winter passing notes to Autumn asking for Summer dates at the
beach.
Spring planting the best seeds for Autumn, all the while Summer rolls
its eyes.
Autumn from across the year making bursts of color displays
Begging Winter to help them create the most beautiful sunrise
In every variety of hues across the sky creating gorgeous arrays.
The seasons turn in jealousy to the sun and moon
Those celestial beings up in the heavens
To this curse those two are immune
At least they have an eclipse sometimes, one that leaves impressions.
All of this over the course of a year, seasons never crossing borders
Love cast apart on each side,
Relying on each other to pass messages to the others
If they were reunited it'd be chaos, you can understand why.
Snow during a hurricane and blossoms in a snowstorm
Crops crying out for water, but receiving none

It's the order of things, the way it was formed
Once they might have known each other, but those days long since are
done.
All the seasons on four corners of the world
Commanded never to cross the threshold
Marking their territories clear with their elements unfurled
Only in those sectors, they are able to withstand it. You could say each
time of year is climate controlled.
It makes me wonder what each season did
To endure a punishment such as this:
Across from their lover for all eternity, their meeting, heaven forbid
Living in long lost love from afar, forever in agony but also in bliss.

I'm the One That Got Away

I'm tired of playing second string to your list of priorities
I'm slowly becoming okay with that,
Soon you won't remember me, I'll just be optional in your memories
I'll be on paper somewhere, not in the third dimension, just flat.
Set me alight and watch my heart burn
Dancing in the midnight rain and feeling the cold in the distance,
Somewhere far off I know my heart is thinking of you while it yearns...
But we aren't talking about you, right now it's my existence.
There is room for me in this world, just not in your heart
I can spread out or change shapes
Follow my own desires. I can be a work of art.
In every mold I'm put I'll find every way to escape.
I'll miss you but I know you're losing interest
I gave myself permission to move on
After awhile your less than bare minimum bore witness
That's okay, you showed me what I can improve on.
I feel like I'm getting left behind
Even though I'm having the best time of my life
Now the opportunity arises to make my life any way I design
I can carve it in any way, using my own knife.
You won't miss me, but I'll ring a bell next time you hear stilettos
This time, I'll give you a kiss to put us right
Sometimes you have to let go
This time, it's my life. This time, I'm saying goodnight.

Beauty Refined

Day and night I dream of you and every time it dulls my senses
Like an addict wanting more than just your presence
You come around and my body lowers its defenses
I get lost at the thought of you, it's almost more than pleasance.
When you're gone I go through withdrawals
My body goes to war in attempt to find you and ease my quarrels
We're just two people navigating life like explorers
Writing down rights and wrongs making our own morals.
My body is drawn to yours like they belong together every season
No matter the place as long as it spans across any region
Breathing in the scent of your skin, but every breath feels like treason
I can't lose you, you're my very reason.
Traveling the world with you sounds like more than wonder
Standing out of rains way, watching you but listening to the thunder
There's nothing to fear when we're the hunters
Even when it seems like we're outnumbered.
Serenity feels more like a happy ending without "The End"
You don't have to try too hard to see we'll be happy, there's nothing to
mend
Your every need and want is something I'll tend
I'll make the sun rise just so I can see you happy to attend.
Something tells me you'll always be running through my mind
Any future we build will just be combined
It's like beauty meshed together, a precious metal refined
Something that can only happen if the stars were to align.

Compassionate

It's amazing how you create an irreducible minimum
No mind games or immaturity,
The thought of you is like sipping on warm cinnamon
You're something once in a lifetime, maybe the century.
Proper treatment sounds so pompous
I guess at least when I say it aloud,
But you make no hesitation on any promise
None you make to me at least, you don't cease to make me proud.
We don't automatically know how to love someone
We learn how to love each other, it's a process
It's not a talent you can just summon
It's not a difficult thing to grasp, this whole concept.
People turn love into what they feel
How they've been treated before comes into relevance.
They complicate it until it's no longer ideal
It's expected to be perfect or every notion to have elegance.
Romance isn't always you waiting with a surprise
But it's the little things that add up,
Like how you wake me up because you know I love the sunrise
Or when you miss me you don't hesitate to catch up.
He loves me, he loves me not
It's not all flowers and daisies
He loves me, will we tie the knot?
It's not unsurety when you're in your eighties.
It's the calm in the calamity

The steadiness through the storm
Creating an escape but present in reality
Sharing your heart and keeping them warm.
It's steady and always benign
It's me keeping you safe until the end of time.

Amorevole

Like a tune that resonates with my ear
A note that plays, somehow only I can hear.
That note, that melody is your song.
A beautiful stroke of genius reverberating through the air can do no
wrong.
Maybe I have high hopes that when I hear it you'll appear
If the song gives any indication you'll be equally strong.
It's not an ordinary tune or ballad
It has a whimsy air to it, flowing and then growing rapid
All in a good pace. Casually listening you can't miss one note
The song intently listening to every word your heart wrote
All of those insights, declaring them valid
Yours as well as mine, as the ink does devote.
As if on the violins of our hearts playing pizzicato
The only stopping point is to grab the bow and play vibrato
Tugging on our hearts strings leading us closer than ever
Those steel strings are strong, never to sever
This song pairs specifics, a matchmaking aficionado
You now tuned my ear to the song, how clever.

~The Grey Area~

In the Woods

Here I lay
Deep in the chilled woody autumn
Unsure whether I am the predator or the prey
My consciousness is within me, somewhere at the very bottom
I feel as Snow White
Eyes unopened, body barely movable
Not knowing dusk from twilight
I hear you in the distance, looking for me as per usual.

Here I lay on this oak table
In a dress barely fit for the season,
Wishing how this were all a fable
And wondering, "what is your very reason?"
I'm here because of you, in a state of paralysis.
I shiver as the breeze graces my skin
Are you my ally or my nemesis?
I'll know when we meet if you're my savior or his twin.
Here I lay draped in a white sun dress
Hair long as I've been here lay near my hips
The leaves don't touch me, but the surroundings lay such a mess
Bursting with color same as my lips.
I stay true to myself, hands folded neatly
Goosebumps on my skin, I wish I dressed warmer
I'd have restless legs but I can't move freely.
How did I get here? I can't remember anything former.

Here I lay knowing you'll find me, and I'll awake when you do
Each day you grow closer
I hear the leaves rustle, it must be you.
I do hope you're not my opposer.

64

I hear the white noise of the wind
It circles around me taking the leaves with it
I can't open my eye, not even to squint.
There's a nervousness growing I must admit.
I'm here because of you, don't know why
But you grow close, I feel your time coming nigh.
I have to lay here unmoving, until you wake me up bit by bit.
When we meet I must declare you guilty, until your deeds I may
acquit.

Winter Woods

It's not a dream, and I'm still here.
The leaves fall around me
I await you, and you still draw near.
I lay motionless by slumber, eyes closed and unable to see.
I stay here more, the trees grow bare.
I had a dream of my surroundings:
Leaves no more, yet the sky so fair.
I hear you in the distance, my heart still pounding.
It's not a dream and I am chilled by frost
Snow never to be touched falls gently around me
The wily wind knows me, not at all lost.
To me the cardinals sing their winter songs gleefully.
I know it's not your time, but I hear you in the distance:
Your romping through the snow in insistence.
You know where I lay,
You have a journey to surpass but here I stay.
It's not a dream and I'm prepared for the season clad in black,
Save for silver buttons and fur lined boots that would sound a
click-clack.
Is it a funeral or a fashion statement?
You're coming to me, I'd solely be in my element.
You are the stranger, who are you anyway?
Reveal yourself, this place seems an everlasting day.
Are you for me or against my cause?
Be clear as I'd rather not dwell on the inconsistency that was.

It's not a dream and I'm unable to awake.
I lay in stillness with no pronounced movement
I long to move and stretch, there is so much at stake
After all you may view this and find amusement.
Break the spell and wake me up
Come quickly, I pray you not be a creeping buttercup.
Fulfill our destinies and go your route,
Don't grow roots to watch and sprout.

It's not a dream and I'm unsure of your intentions
You could be the right or wrong one to wake me, now that you
mention.
We may duel until the everlasting sun sets,
We may find comfort in knowing there are no regrets.
Indulge my curiosity and show me how I will wake.
Is it our connection or your very presence,
The whole essence that will open my eyes as daybreak?
To find out is the future, the present must have patience.

~Chapter of Impermeable Darkness~

My Immortal

My immortal, immortality, you uninspire me to write.
How I see you destroy, you prowl the earth to its very ends.
I see you in my mind day and through the night:
You're never content, not once wanting to make amends.
In what way do you not tarry?
You idle, yet all at once blaze through leaving destruction in your path.
We're on different times, you've lasted through the ages and I've not.
I'm still debating on whether or not that's scary.
Destruction is your name, and all caring not of the consequences, you
leave everyone else to feel your wrath.
How do I hate you? Let me count the ways:
Ten thousand and one, the power and strength you crave.
You have no hold, you're only held by your delusions.
Captives you call them, but you're the only one captive. That is, to your
own mental illusions.
Now I must away with an awesome heart,
Remember my big words whilst we're apart.

The Power of Invisibility

Invisibility, that one ability that only select few have.
I know what you're thinking, "How peaceful it must be!"
My friend, you're wrong in more ways than one. Words like that feel
like only a jab.
How it feels is the ice on your skin, the wind breaking in, alone!
Alone. Lost at sea.
Nobody sees you, not even your loved ones.
Crystallized is all you are, only you may view how your tears of glass
flee.
Don't break under the pressure, after all, it's only seven tons.

Hitman

Prim, proper, and neat
Not one hair out of place, laugh should you think an easy feat.
Formal clothes pressed tightly
Buttons lined up and necktie knotted rightly.
Shoes shined and check the morning air
Lace them perfectly just as the other pairs.
Make no mistake, this is no small task
Put yourself in another's shoes, you only have to ask.
Walk the grounds and stay in boundaries,
Respect the elders and each place they put foundries.
Do the work and perfect your skills,
Pay the others no mind or they'll give you the chills.
Hide in your room waiting for someone to ask
Go put on a brave face, grab the mask.
Blend into the crowd and sight your target
You have an assignment, this isn't a night market.
Stalk and hide in the shadows you must
In there, follow them inside to gain their trust.
A recognized facade, assumed identity
Smile and wave don't show them anxiety
Let them have their cake and eat it too
You didn't do any wrong, but if only you knew.

Patience for a Promise

"A little bit longer," you say. "Soon, very soon. Even sooner."
I have what I need, but am constantly crushed emotionally.
Months go by. Enough. Is this just a rumor?
My eyes blur with tears, I wish it wasn't woefully.
When will it be my turn to have peace, prosperity, and all?
You want the best for me, I know this true.
Yet I can't help but think, is this some sick game of yours in which you
see me fall?
To every direction I look, the only one facing me is you.
Silence fills the air. Speechless, the both of us.
Painful, watchful, scornful, hopeful: a stir of emotions all at once.
I feel like if we were to talk, there would be too much to discuss.
So we sit there in wait, the air heavy. Not air, almost like a substance.
Fire, like smoke to the lungs burning my soul.
The anticipation is weighty, just end it now.

Forever Out of Reach

Hand reaching out and grasping
Yet cold air rushing through my hand so ghastly.
Barely seen and a phantom of the night
Where are you, my love, that I delight?
So far yet so near
Even next to me we feel separated by years,
Here and gone through the day
I lie awake wondering if you'll stay away.
Mist in the darkness and I know:
You're here, never late, never to go.
Hiding in the corner bashful and true
Oh how I wish I could be your rescue.
Trapped in a world between ours
I'm helpless against your hold on me, your powers.
Gone in an instant and reappearing the next,
My heart and mind you do solely vex!
Hide my fears deep in my heart
My body aches desperately knowing we're apart.
Break my spirit and poach my air
Caress my face with your loving flair.
A cold brush against my arm
Your fingers tracing my blood-flow like some kind of charm.
Your light is fading and I'm not sure why
How I miss you, my phantom of the night.
Kiss me through the night and haunt my dreams

Let it playback in my mind as a requiem.
Salt burns my skin, that's what tears are made of
Leaving wakes of destruction in remembrance of my beloved
phantom.

The Scouting Wolf

You who watch and observe
Who is it really that you serve?
I sense your monstrous desire
To so hang me higher and higher,
Why do you feel this way? What have I done that you scout my life,
And cause me to walk in all the ways of strife?
I see you little wolf, twisting and turning your head at my every move
I anticipate your lunge and attack, I was gifted this life. It's not for you
to take and abuse.
I anticipate this all indeed, only for you to walk away
Is it possible you were just a stray?
No, not even, I wish. A scout for sure. The direction you're heading, I
remember. I know your master.
That awful romancer, clothed with darkness around. He wants my life
and not even the latter.
As you go back to your master and give your status report
Tell him that he has no choice, my life is not going to be cut short.

Deceit in Numbers

Here I was thinking you were harmless, gone even.
When you had intent all along. One not for good, but harm.
You've received a new mission
I'm really trying, struggling to find how I'm wrapped up in your
charm.
I'm disgusted by you, not one emotion towards you is beautiful.
I'm so angry I don't want to let you back in.
What am I, silver that gets put through the crucible?
You're a wolf, and wolves come in numbers, why would I let you- your
pack in?
You were just a scout. You watched at first,
But things changed and you went back to your master in that dark
alley.
Right now? For my blood you hunger and thirst.
I know I'm stuck here, in my "safe place" while you have time to rally.
Where to hide, where to go? I know what comes after you go.
When you return, there will be multitudes of ravenous beasts
All different, but from the same dark grove.
One will come forward, and offer cleistes.
I won't take it, no not a one.
I must stand my ground, and wait while you snarl.
If I were to go with you, my love and life as I know it would be gone.
I'm staying here. You're wasting your breath by bothering to gnarl.
I stay standing, exactly where I am.
Watching and waiting for that grand caravan.

I know you're a person to wait, and wait you must.
You're the one who started this. You've lost my trust.

Breakaway From the Pack

How fitting it is- that darkness you wear as a cloak,
I'm unsure if I'll be able to speak up or if I'll choke.
It hides you so perfectly, your facade is unbreakable.
I don't know what you are, but it's you. You're unmistakable.
I couldn't figure you out, I hesitated. I was forced to pause.
You have a pattern, I saw it before I knew what it was:
Flirtation, palpitations, frustration, manipulation.
Me? I was your fixation!
It hurt learning the truth.
How was I supposed to know you've done this from youth?
You traitor! You were never on my side.
Smile fake as you like, I know it's snide.
You saw my heart, and that's what drew you to me
You prey on people- especially the ones with empathy.
You don't know me, that's the thing.
Intuition I'll never ignore, even when it stings.
You are where you are, there you shall stay
Here I am in my little circle, my peace, my safe space.
I'm not leaving or stepping outside,
Try as you might, and I know you will, I'm staying- you can step aside.

The Hunter and His Prey

That took a turn for the worse
You know the story is downhill,
When it's only the first verse
Well, they say shoot to thrill.
I know why the arrow got so close
You were aiming for my heart,
But I'm the only one who knows
You're both despicable and a work of art.
Rotten apples!
Because of you I can't even look at a chapel.
Bittersweet!
Ridiculous, you aren't even discreet.
That arrow came too close
I'm in the woods and you're right at home.
You wolf, you heathen
Staring down the tip of your arrow makes it hard to breathe in.

Guide Through the Path

In what twisted works, in what world is this okay?
I'm not sure if I can run the race, or even gather strength to stay.
Can't I catch a break, or even a measly breath?
I refuse to do this, everything about it screams death.
Shall I go or shall I stay?
Maybe we can go together, it'd be easier, anyway.
A new life beckons from the horizon
If you're afraid, worry not! For on me, you may keep your eyes on.
We're at a fork in the road, be aware
Don't look to the left or right, you may find yourself scared.

Beauty or the Beast?

Your beauty is astounding. You're perfect and breathtaking in every
aspect.
Under your skin are the scales of a serpent, and through your veins run
through most poisonous venoms.
I can't look away, a glowing radiance emits from you! I have nothing
with me to deflect.
Beneath that glow is an evil intent, a harsh truth- ruthless malice is the
reason you're phenom.
I love you, and I want to spend eternity by your side.
Eternity will be short for me if I go with you, resist while I still can.
Ropes burn my wrists as I look into your precious golden flecked eyes.
I need to run, my heart pounds and my eyes sting. It was over- all of it!
Everything before it began.
Beautiful, smart, hilarious, strong.
Disgusting, stubborn, angry, all wrong!
How can I hate you when I'm so relentlessly and hopelessly in love?
Am I really entranced by your love, or the lack thereof?

Beauty vs the Beast

Where do I go from here?
I'm stuck between two worlds.
A fork in my path, two people are near
Around me does mist of confusion furl.
Right and wrong, two beautiful representatives at each end
In reality the Beauty is pain and suffering.
The Beauty is the Beast that grows and ascends.
Discerning is infinitely puzzling.
Which is good and which bad?
I look between them trying to make a choice
One wears armor, but why is beauty ironclad?
I hope I don't lose my voice.

False Hope

I'm waiting on you
I can't tell what you're thinking
I'm ashamed to say I wish it weren't true
You're so distant, so far away! I feel like I'm sinking.
Lower and lower I go, waiting
When will you be there?
I only had eyes for us, but now it all feels weighty.
I can't even gasp for air.
You know where to find me should you ever feel the need,
At the bottom of my heart that feels like a raging ocean.
I'll be waiting, please take heed.
Save me, if you ever have the notion.

Heartbreak Heathen

You and I have a love hate numb relationship
With you? Oh for you, my heart is relentlessly in love.
With my mind under your control my conscience is filled with hate,
I love you with everything in me and everything else thereof.
Emotion and logic battle so often that it's hard to concentrate.
I try to stay away from you with everything I am
As much as I try, I don't think I can.
I hide because you deserve so much better
It feels forbidden, but from past loves I know you're still bitter.
You're so sweet, it's a toxic sweet.
Sugar to the lips and poison to the soul.
I can't run from you, I don't want defeat.
Rip out my heart, and replace it with coal.

Battle Against the Masses

Bleak darkness above and in surrounding hills
Here am I deep in the valley surrounded by black mist
Those dark creatures lurking and watching they did mull
Crepuscular figures of tar, blackness, and bones snap towards me and
creep in a twist.
Such bleak vision I have, of the mist and clouds around
I stand in my safety, anchored in the fray.
I know their intentions well, to put me beneath the ground.
I'm not going or stepping outside of my safety, my circle. I'm prepared,
come what may.
A million to one are the chances you see,
but I have the strength of a million, and millions on my side.
You don't believe me? Watch how these dastardly hellhounds flee.
No, this in this protection, my protection, I abide.
Tell us! Tell us more!
No, I know your plans. I know the secrets of the light, for that is from
where I come.
You? You're doomed to the darkness from which you came, for
evermore!
I rebuke you, and scorn you. Stay away from me. What, did you think
I was dumb?
Stay back, decrepit beast!
You gather to form one being, not a fleet!
Try as you might, I'm not yours to devour.
I'm in control of my destiny nobody else gets to choose the hour.

Rooting for Me

For you I disappoint
I can't look into the sadness of your eyes.
I hate my actions, after me you did anoint.
I look at you but not for long, I can't speak lies.
Get me out of this, I struggle my worst,
I'm bound and stuck on my own.
For your spirit I hunger and thirst.
I miss you, how you made me feel like home.
Your presence alone speaks numbers
The multitudes cheer within me.
All this but my spirit slumbers,
I miss you and what I would see.
I try to find you but I'm lost in mystery
The fog and the mist all black around—
I know where I'm at, I've seen it in dreams' history.
This is truly scary, there's trouble abound.
I did this to myself, I try to stay steadfast
I know your command triumphs, the beginning, middle, and the
everlast.

Life's Fragility

I'm hanging on by a thread,
And that thread is on fire.
I can't seem to get ahead
Nothing ever seemed so dire.
I slip and sway,
Try as I might, the flame won't dwindle.
There's no use, I'll never get away
Everything I do is used to kindle.
The fire is for a crucible
But I'm not a precious stone,
Put me through it, but I'm not reusable.
All those efforts to make me tougher will leave you alone.
I'm not iron or steel,
I bend and break.
I may not be valuable but I'm still real,
I'm here, and I'm not fake.
You can't mold and shape me,
I come as I am.
You can't take as you please, I'm not free.
As far as I can see, nobody gives a damn.

Expletive For an Adversary

Sometimes I wonder why I was given this life,
It hurts to live it with the people around me.
These people are filled solely with strife
Don't misunderstand, it's not the end of me, not yet at least
Sometimes I wish it were the end of them,
Or the very least let my adversaries reap what they sow.
Hear the innocent's cry, then
Make the men of evil regret what they know.
Drink their poison and let them have it
A taste of their own medicine, their dirty habit.
Take their hearts should they exist,
And send them down into the endless abyss.
Turn the tides and stir the waters red,
Make their loved ones never to wed.

Love is Poison

Pop the cork and hum a tune
Pick a vial, this one chosen specifically by you.
A vivacious color, glimmering in the light
Specks of brightness swirling around the vial are my delight.
Such beauty that is unfailing
Like a thick liquid glitter swishing and swaying.
Love drunk, drink down
Look away, don't be tempted by the false crown.
It's impossible! Loves first sight is compulsion
It's not real, that demulsion.
What a sweet taste to the lips!
A warmth. A promise of heat in the cold.
Smoothly it goes down, memorable as a kiss.
Heart palpation and adrenaline to my veins, a promise of gold.
A smile creeps upon my face, a happiness
Like butterflies in my torso
I float aimlessly at your sight unaware of your craftiness
A taste of sweetness lingers, or I thought so.
Sweet, Bittersweet, then bitter.
Heartbeat quickens until it breaks
A sour turn of the stomach, must be the glitter?
Weakness to my bones, fallen to my knees, a heart for the stake.
The cold hard floor becomes lukewarm as I freeze.
Mine apothecary, a mistake! Please!
Why had the poison my name on it from the shelf above?

I did no wrong, I only fell in love.

91

Locomotive

Insistently press on, go forward endlessly,
Set on the path of destiny.
Every path planned and taken with caution
Even vulnerable you're still impermeable and brazen.
The pressure to coal turns it to diamonds
As the fire purifies the beauty of gold.
No need to take care around the bends,
Only follow the blueprints as they unfold.
Make haste and stay on the tracks
Full steam ahead
Trailblazing through the tunnel and never looking back
Like fate to a string and needle to a thread.
Fire of determination to the brim as a locomotive
Both unique and similar to others, closely derivative.
Release the work of passion as smoke billows behind
Keep ahead of the smoke lest you in your own environment be blind.

Villainous Heartbreak

Love is an illusion
Listen close, you'll soon come to the same conclusion.
Take caution not to fall into delusion
It doesn't bring you closer, but into seclusion.
That true love you see is a lie
Like moths are butterflies of the night.
Let's talk about true love's kiss
How every single one we get we're supposed to miss.
Love at first sight only leaves you cross
Every 'princess' pet name, but when have you waltzed?
Go get swept off your feet, try me.
The thing you'll be left sweeping is the chimney.
A rose by any other name would still be thorny
You don't hold the pen to your life, but go ahead. Write your love
story.
Scribble away at this and that,
Don't you dare talk to me. I don't speak chicken scratch.
Oh no, dear. You, I tried to warn.
Pluck those flower petals, looking forlorn.
He loves me, he loves me not
When was the last time he looked at you? Or have you since forgot?
As a mere bridesmaid has second thoughts,
So does the one you let possess your enamored nature
Overlook it, be my guest. Over the mistakes paint the gloss
In a heartless frostbite let those thoughts be encaptured.

Please, by all means!
Practice your needlework while he cooks up his schemes.
A housewife is as silent as a church mouse
He wants to rule, it's his house.
Keep waiting, your I think I see your knight in shining armor
Sorry, that's just the elderly farmer.
Oh brave and dashing young prince,
She'll be a spinster if you don't come since.

I don't mock, I tell only truth
I think I see a grey hair! Oh dear, please fancy your youth.
I mean to say, there's no point in waiting
He has his pick of the patch, he's looking and debating.
Wake up and smell the flower you so pick
You'll thank me when you realize none stay through thin and thick.
Look around, don't be foolish!
Child, what man do you see who isn't brutish?
Dear, I'm sorry things changed,
I only tried to protect you, not prevent vows exchanged.
Look at me! Say my name.
I see you wed and things aren't the same.
I spoke from experience and trust no more
This is everything I've ever known, ever before.
I lost sight of love and romantic affection
I remain alone, I'm just your fear's reflection.

War of Wits

Oh melancholy melody
My everything, my dynamic revolves around thee
From heroic endeavors
Attract darkness that only the sword can sever.
Hear in my mind a solemn tune
Watch into the night leaning on the windowsill,
Up at the sky imagine the dark side of the moon
Don't flinch when the wind blows and sends a chill.
A beautiful tune so dark and strong
Listen to the rumbles of the orchestra throng,
Uplifting but holding the evil in its place
Along the wooden tree lines, my fingers trace.
Hold fast through the storm and place your trust
Brush away each piece of dust
Leave it with the town you aim to leave
Take not one piece of them, you don't owe them, not one thing you
received.
The strength of the war drums low and steady flow
Each warning horn exhibiting intense power from just one blow
War in my mind and a feat of endurance,
Only there would foes surrender to us.
The dirge plays in case the thunder peals too early.
A line up of an opponent's army turns the tide surly,
Battle cry and charging force
Tell a courageous tale and don't reveal the source.

A mourning for an innocent life but a joy of resurrection
These wars exist only through my reflection
The battle was lost but the war hasn't been taken
In every unsettling infliction I wage war until I mentally awaken.
You're my only saving grace.
You, my conscience, remind me each battle doesn't seal my fate.
My song and my strength endless
Never leave, you'll be defenseless.
Return to your first instinct, your first home
Where we battle as gladiators in ancient Rome.

Inferno's Domain

In the heat of the moment
There is no time to analyze, to look at every component.
Seize the day, carpe diem as they call it
It's never that easy, no one will ever admit.
Run through fire
Mind your life on the line, how survival is dire
Beat through flames.
It's for the best, should you come out entirely changed.
Think you're done?
A sorry mistake, it's not even begun.
You haven't seen anything yet
Look up to see what the sky has soon to beget.
Plumes of fire rain down from heaven
There is no hiding, it's out of the question.
Take cover as solar flares come down
Every tree and shrub, all the foliage the fire drowned.
Consuming only in specifics
At least that's what you're led to believe as the fire crashes over the land
as the Pacific.
Muscles flexed and blood pressure spiked
Your hair stands on its ends, lightning strikes.
Pillars of flames miss you narrowly
It's now or never, run in and be baptized by fire thoroughly.
Almost as lava the waves grow turbulent

Grab a trident and rule your domain, make whirlpools a vivacious current.

99

Raw and Unthawed

Sorrow is a coldness washing over my body
Far as the eye can see the sky grows dark, and the weather foggy.
A buildup of blood behind my cheeks,
Nature never touched leaves overflowing creeks.
Inspiring tears to flood my eyes
I've heard when it rains is when angels cry,
But my tears were destined to never fall
I can't cry if I'd never had you, after all.
A cover for my eyes and a numbness to my mind
Lost in the woods is a similar feeling, confusion by design.
Sadness clings to me like wet clothes in the rain,
However; there is no rain. Only fog and bewilderment remain.
Chills are unable to resist the urge to run down my spine
Frozen mud and mire below my feet, above barren tree branches
intertwine.
Unfeigned tingling courses through my veins
Not even layers keep out the cold, yet my calefaction remains.
Pangs of pain radiate as my chest aches
Hold my heart closer and meditate on time's past mistakes.
Serotonin's chemical rival leaves me burned along my odyssey
Acting as my inhibitor, but in selfishness uses my happiness as
commodity.
Sadness washes over me like ice freezes over water
A mournful escapade led by a marauder.
This was bound to happen

In the fires of love did my heart so blacken.
I felt it deep within my bones
I was being dragged into my own emotions by my choice of
millstones!
Dread brings me to my knees
Arteries pumping blood rushing from my heart at zero degrees.
Heart frozen over, the doctor's decree:
Frozen at the time when I knew you weren't the one for me.

Digestive Heart

I feel so lost
Like I never really belonged,
Especially to part of your life
I feel like everything I did was pointless, each thing ended in strife.
When you did something for me I felt more empty than alive
Like I'm left to pick up the pieces and try to survive.
You never looked at me like I looked at you
Even when you gave me attention I was see through.
I looked at you like you were part of my world
I left my heart to you not realizing how badly I wanted it returned,
And you looked at me like I was just part of the script
I was an actress you didn't see as fully equipped.
I'll never be enough for you, or anything you want.
You treat others better than me and treat the situation as nonchalant.
You say you love me but in the same breath take it back
In each instance it feels like you support a heart attack.
I put in extra effort and labor to help
You took everything I made and used it solely for yourself,
But you wouldn't even lift a finger for me if it meant sparing your
energy
Acting as if the very thought of me gave you lethargy.
But you couldn't be bothered to think of me anyways,
When I support and cheer you on through any phase.
I wonder what wicked scheme goes through your mind
All that's lovely and good of you goes through mine.

Maybe at first I put you on a pedestal,
Overlooking so much and claiming you were incredible.
I have your best interest at heart and you continue to string me along!
I thought you had mine too, but how I was so very wrong.
Is this all a game to you?
You charm for a few wins, now you leave nothing for review.
Every day at first you treated my heart as a precious stone
Kept it under lock and key because it was the most expensive thing
you owned.

Now you use it like a sport
Going back and forth and displaying how I fall short,
You take back everything you used to say and do
My nights are occupied wishing on shooting stars for my rescue.
I don't know what to believe or how hurt I should be
When you took my hand and made me believe it was destiny,
It's like you'd act on life saving surgery only to alter my parts
To examine and study in my chest the bleeding heart.
Take what you like and leave what you don't
Treating me if you could choose love is what hurts the most.
Draw blood while singing with me, arm in arm.
Shushing me with each scratch when I sense reason to be alarmed.
I don't remember being a patron of the hearts,
Especially when it's not reciprocated with a refusal to be as beautiful as
art.
Composed art is complicated and at times scary to make
But at least it's genuine, not one bit of it is fake.
If you can't do this, step aside for someone who can
A love untoxic that can make me feel worthy again.
What am I supposed to believe?
Yours is a love I was never meant to receive.

Without a Loss

I felt drained, like my social battery died.
Cried the whole day so I could sleep the whole night,
Fainting and losing consciousness
Causing such a spectacle unless I keep it to myself, my goodness.
Stop waiting for a sign,
I realize their lack of interest and confusion is one, not benign.
Letting go is mourning something I never had
It's a loss of appetite, an isolation that makes me feel unworthy. Just a
tad.
It's not that I don't care for you
The issue I take is with your antics, all of them untrue.
Yet my understanding only reaches so far
Why can't I be without you? You'd leave such a detrimental scar.

Restricted Afflicted

Don't send them a good morning
It'll be all the more informing.
Let them come to you,
Should they ever do.
As you said, "okay, goodnight, sleep well"
A sweet notion at first, but you had a story to tell.
That is what you call a nothing sandwich to the public
Oh the next day you were quiet, but trying to lay it on thick.
Telling others I meant nothing to you
No! Please, go on. Tell me more, how I should've knew.
And you had no problem saying it
All of that hurt way more than I'll ever admit.
You claim to have anyone you want so you string me along,
Go ahead, sing someone else your stupid love song.
Take me for granted,
But still I hope they don't treat you like you treat me, I even demand it.
I thought I loved you, but this isn't what I wanted
You don't make an effort to talk, you've only responded.
When you have a lack of attention is when you beg for mine
If you get bored you take up my time.
Is this what I deserve?
Not even close, I know someone will treat me like I need to be
preserved.
You don't get it- I don't want them, I just want you to see:
I want you to do better for me.

But you won't, so I will.
While wishing you would, I've already mastered the skill.
Note to myself:
You don't belong in a box on someone's shelf,
Learn your lesson
Read between the lines or look into their heart- stop the imaginary
tension.

Chronic Fatigue

My muscles weaken
Their lack of tension only deepens
Heartbeat slows down,
Breathing slow and heavy as I look around.
Cold flows over me
My senses feel as if they've been lost to sea,
Like I'm out in the storm
Making me wish I would finally be warm.
Bleary-eyed and stumbling
Rickety floorboards recreate my steadiness humbling.
Slowly I make my way
Leaving a gentle chaos in my wake,
To a rest like no other
A cozy silence with a warm cover.
Head drooping and falling occasionally
As one does in their dozing, traditionally.
Swaying and off balance
Take it slow. Of this I'm not callous.
Leaning against walls and nearby support
Using anything within my reach as an escort.
Each step comes with insecure hesitation
Tripping over myself to reach my destination
Attempting to stand straight and tall
In avoidance of taking one last fall.
Leaning down and rolling into place

A warmth finally rushing to my face,
Pulling the blankets up to my neck and getting stable
The one place I can truly be comfortable.

109

To Speak Volumes

Tightness appearing in my chest
A continuous tension test,
Like a knot someone continues pulling
Past the point of its needing securing.
As if cinder blocks weigh me to the bottom of the ocean
Attempting to resurface but the water around me is thick with
emotions.
They say actions speak louder than words,
Yours leave me grappling to come to terms.
What have you been saying to me?
Let me think so we can see.
Let's recount
Here we find out everything you did and take it into account.
Tell me where I'm wrong, but you can't recant
You can't replace it, this isn't a transplant.
Not your actions at least, those ring true.
What are you scared of? Right now we're both see through.
Let's start off with your ignorance
After you got me hooked you began your indifference.
Shall I say, this is astounding:
You do all of this, but you still leave my heart pounding.

A Mourning and a Grievance

It's been a year of your absence
When you left I couldn't find my balance.
I'm sorry that you're gone
The silence in your trek leaves me processing and withdrawn.
You make me determined, I miss you a lot
I really hope you don't think I forgot.
In truth I wish you were still here
There's not one day I don't think about you resisting my own tears.
My heart dies begging it to be a rumor
For things not to end the way they did, that I had noticed sooner.
That I had a better chance to say goodbye.
To beg God for a chance to grab the strings and untie.
I wish you would've had a proper funeral,
That the effects would have been suitable.
I wish we were better to you, that I could've done more.
That I could've picked every flower with you and explored.
I know who to blame, but I wish it was natural
I sob knowing to them you were just collateral.
You were a natural at life, you lived it to its fullest.
To the fullest extent, you always loved us- you checked the boxes on
every list.
You had the biggest heart I've ever met.
I miss you, and I remember you. I promise you I won't forget.

Society Scorned

To pretend I don't exist one moment and that I'm your entire world
the other
As if my seldom breath is purposed to smother.
Be vivacious to everyone else but treat me as if I were a commoner
Put me under lock, key, and guard.
Act like you're my moon and stars,
But you're missing a fact so crucial
That I'm the sun
And it's inevitable to be on opposite spectrums.
Such boldness you speak with when I refuse to please
When you act like I'm a heavy burden, not even one of the least.
Gravity pulling me backwards, or maybe it's destiny
Besides, it's away from you most definitely.
I wish this weren't the case
That you'd give me an ounce of the attention I crave
It was never meant for you to be perfect
To be kind and honest- the society I'd expect,
But to try in every way that matters.
I know you could
I just wish you would.

Mind Games

How is this fair when everything seems hopeless?
Looking into your eyes I get my confirmation: you may be soulless.
You say one thing and act another
"I'll own up to my actions" Never.
Not once with you. It's not fair to me
For you to sit there feeling ecstasy,
While I'm broken and feeling drowned.
I'm beneath you it seems.
Condemned never to surface
Like holding me under water is your only purpose.
Is that what it is, or is it waterboarding?
Sadistic menace, to you this seems rewarding.
Giving me gasps of air until you change your mind again
You'll keep changing your mind until the end of time, indecisive even
then.
Like summer and winter each twice a day.
You're your own opposite, not one emotion stays.
Reading was always my strong suit
I didn't realize that doing it outside of books was a mental dispute.
Open my eyes and see our reflection,
I cannot be this desperate for your attention.
Act like I'm at fault but you're the one holding me captive
I'm not staying forever, I won't continue playing adaptive.

Fanciful Fear

Is this worth it? Are you worth it?
The worry you put me through
I should move on, should time permit
Maybe you won't even notice I withdrew.
The being left on read, being ignored, indirect insults
I'm not finding it to be worth the trouble or the pain.
Mentally mature please, we're all adults
No need to act in vain.
I should move on.
I've been trying so hard for so long
Or even break things off, but it's not easy
The mere thought of it makes me queasy.
I shouldn't be scared of taking a break from you
Chasing peace at this point seems like a fantasy, but you already knew
I was needing time for myself
Just once in awhile, whenever I felt compelled.
I have this fear, not irrational, that you'll move on
That I'll look up one day and you'll be clear gone
Or find someone more interesting
That I'd be wasting my time by myself, unrelenting.
Maybe that's what you need, maybe that's what *I* need.
For now I'm taking it a day at a time, at our chosen speed.

Living a Lie

Disrespect, disrepair, dilapidated, disappoint, disappear- all of it nigh.
This is what happens when you live a lie.
Stop gas lighting, everyone was there. You can't deny.
You disrespect and in turn get disrespected, and you lose your self
respect
What did you expect?
To magically become someone's favorite project?
Life as you know it falls into disrepair
Nothing makes sense, you can no longer breathe common air.
Slowly but surely, everyone loses the will to care.
Lovers, friends and family. All of those relationships become
dilapidated.
Lying breaks their trust, with your track record it's to be anticipated.
Think before you speak next time, your words don't need to be
exaggerated.
Their thoughts of you change, expectations disappoint.
Everyone's closeness begins to disjoint.
It's your own fault, you know. Everything you said was purloined.
Where do you go when everyone in your life begins to disappear?
Think next time, communicate truthfully, leave nothing to mishear.
There is no "home" now, there's nothing here.

Revolting Revolution

Have you ever had your mood drop because of someone else?
People say that's not being able to control your emotions
It's like having someone set you on fire and expecting the ice not to
melt,
Supposing you were extraordinary and not worth oceans.
But doing that is like being heartbroken and then suppressing
Someone you care about hurting your feelings,
All of your hard work before your eyes begins regressing
Weathering in a way that undoes all of your healing.
They know how to do it too
They prim and pinch until something has an effect,
Peeling away your layers like dried glue
Like you were only a little test subject.
Finding that weak link, they know how to bend you to their will
Manipulative they pick pieces and see what they can destroy.
Putting substantial pressure on you until you finish being milled
Applauding as if they were a child and you a toy.
Amazing what they do to leave you hollow and empty,
A disgusting display of dominance.
Prompting you to be their acceptee
It's almost surprising to hear of their prominence.
That they really hurt their own people, everything about them.
Actions that are so pungent it makes me queasy just breathing
They aren't worth a cent of the skin God wrapped their bones in,

Pure vile people turning others like them every day more and more, leaves me ever seething.

117

Humanity's Sanctimony

If you have faith in humanity you will be deceived.
They say one thing and do another
Take your time mortal, watch and perceive
What they do not only to themselves, but to their own brother.
Extremely hypocritical of them all
To say love but to hate in their hearts.
Under every crisis they thrive, their determination enthralled
Sadly they create these issues themselves, natural disasters are
seemingly sparse.
An enigmatic creature, that's for sure
Obedience unlocks understanding but that's what they don't get
It's rare to find one person with a heart genuinely pure,
Doing good to them is being seen as a threat.
I'm not sure when they got confused
Or how they thought doing wrong was better than the truth
Go back in time to see what all of their wars did
If you can't find a rarity, it's better to find the nearest exit.

Haunted Memories

The place is yours to explore,
But like lady of the lake or the midnight howler
Adding legends to memories that weren't there before
Stay close, you might have an unlucky encounter.
Harmless things become rigid and rough around the edges
Things so vicious now harmless and joyous.
If that's the case, why must there lay traps and dredges?
Look beyond the illusion, tap into that clairvoyance.
At least that's what the heart feels on the outside
Pathways made semi-safe for crossing, but appearances lie.
That's why the clouds lay low, they have something to hide
Whatever darkness surrounds, it must be darker than it implies.
Plenty of things that don't make sense
Be not afraid, I'll be here when you call.
Something new is usually different, it's alright to feel tense
Not everything here will be exactly as I recall.
Changing the scenery and moving objects
Cursed castles and hexed homes
Navigate the area with just a concept
Watch your step, the ground is not all earthy loam.
People removed and tasks undone
Faces get blurred and events swim in the distance
Carry a lantern, at least until we can find the sun
Only hearts can bring everything into existence.
Matches feeding fire to candles and their wicks

Keep track and cartograph, only some areas have borders.
Walking barefoot in places unknown holding only a candlestick
Welcome to my heart, the most complicated of quarters.

Bradycardia

It's not okay for us to play pretend feelings,
Don't you see that?
I'm at my limit but you broke the ceiling
Somehow this tops all of your crossings, and you do it with great éclat.
Eyes lock and unspoken words ring through the air
The loudest sound I've heard pertaining to quiescence,
Two halves of different purposes, but both equally rare
As two contrasting diamonds with fluorescence.
You're going to give my broken heart a heart attack.
If you're going to break me, do it gently.
Let my crushed heart slip like sand through your fingers slats
Just don't keep it, you can't put it in a jar and pretend to be friendly.
Doing something so terrible with such gentleness, somehow makes
you seem courtly.
I'd rather it be soft tears than rough sobs
Maybe quick so I can only be left crying softly,
It's like leaving me in a tower and taking all of the doorknobs.
Hard conversations have to be spoken into existence
A sad knowing as you caress my face
It was inevitable, yet my heart feels a tug of resistance
One last kiss, one last embrace.

Supposed Hamartia

A banquet in celebration tonight
I'm not quite sure why, possibly to gather strengths.
It's almost dizzying, like something is off but not quite
As if someone was infiltrating mental ranks.
Everyone has such a friendly face. They look so nice,
But watching. Almost centering in on my reaction
Not a double take or a mistaken glance twice
Ensuring I act properly or to their satisfaction.
Each person looks familiar but all of them I can't quite place
One after another offering me their dishes.
Any facial expression I can't quite trace
A notable sacrifice I perceive, giving me endless wishes.
The room dims and details fade
Like someone put a filter over my eyes
All of my senses gradually becoming delayed
Very relaxed, noticing no indication of my demise.
Slowly each piece they expect a return
Performing even though the curtain is drawn
Intuition detecting nothing to concern,
Not realizing I am just a pawn.
Wondering why I'm receiving more than I deserve
Dismissing it just as quick when someone pulls me aside
Who remained in the party only to observe
Picking me up and walking away with only a moment to decide.
Wanting to be alert and awake, but I lay limp in your grasp

Wishing I was more al dente than scotta,
Attempted speech but it only comes out a rasp
I'm no more lucid than cheese is terra cotta.
"I was saving you from a dinner host
You didn't know was serving you poison."
You kept watch so I wouldn't turn into a ghost.
I thought I heard you, but I'm too tired to let your voice in.

This entire time I thought I was the hero,
But you were saving me all along.
Timing my rescue before they made me a parasite in vitro
It will haunt me, wondering where everything went wrong.

124

Deforestation

We're all fairies acting without guilt
Not understanding humans or their emotions,
Watch their intricate expressions, it's a poorly knitted quilt.
Creating problems and falling into their own commotions.
Burying their emotions in guilt or shame
Perceiving everyone who doesn't a different breed
With a green thumb and emotionally tame
A gardener who wanders through the heart and scatters the seed.
Head held high and enter with decorum
We're surprisingly resilient, trust me I know
Some more than others, just as select trees change colors in autumn
It's like planting a tree upside down and it still grows.
The thing is that the roots still grow
They grow as branches without any leaves
It begs curiosity of what goes on below:
What then, grows underneath?
Do the branches then grow as leaves underground?
Maybe they replace the roots never to foliage again,
It sticking to a specific system in its compound
Secrets engraved on the leaves, each one hidden underneath but
written in pen.

Burning Burden

I don't feel heard or seen
There's a point that makes me break and there's no in between.
The ship can't avoid the ice,
And suddenly whatever I do can't suffice.
Asteroids hurtling towards earth,
And you aren't the savior of the story
Everyone depends on you, but this scales your worth.
You aren't even the main character, you're just part of the inventory.
I'm the very start of me
Designing my future and working hard
They are the end of me- everything I wanted to be.
All for the rest of the world to takes me in and give the lowest regards.
How they look down on me, the world patronizing.
Everyone who's sight I enter utter against me any curse
I'd say every, but I'm not like them, I'd never resort to scrutinizing.
I'll tell the story backwards if I need, I promise it's not rehearsed.
Life is meant to be enjoyed and lived to its fullest
Now it seems that everyone wants a serving of what you have, they feel
the need to measure.
We should live in the present, not go through life as a tourist
That takes away the beauty of the earth, the pleasure.
It sounds ridiculous but the world is heavy
I may not be Atlas holding it forever,
But it has weight without the judgment of others already.
You can't cut off others without feeling the burn of the sever.

Marble Under the Moon

Sculpting me, I carefully come to form
Chiseling every inch of marble until I'm born.
Day and night I see you toil
Under the moonlight my carving boils.
The flecks of color shimmer in the limestone
As I curl my fingers into the moonlight shone,
Across the room you lie asleep
My torso and arms are done but my legs are not formed to leap.
Daylight comes and I am still once more
Hard at work for the 2nd month in a row, but who's keeping score?
Attention to detail, you have a talent to be commended
It's as the drapery hugs me just as you intended.
Your hands raw and bandaged, waking you up through the night
This is my chance to reveal my animation, to see your delight.
After expressed tranquility I finally win you over,
Presenting a mirror to me, beauty enough to make a drunk man sober.
"Sleep tight, don't mind the monsters above your bed,"
You speak crudely of the gargoyles overhead.
Dismiss it nonetheless, beauty is my jurisdiction
In the attraction and virtue of mine there is no contradiction.
Daybreak spills in that I'm frozen in place
No matter my position I'm the epitome of grace.
After filing and sanding I'm so close to finished,
The moon rises leaving me rough, but it doesn't reflect my beauty or
diminish.

You're sleeping again, taking a break when I could be polished
No matter, the tools in my hands will leave him astonished.
Furious you take the buffer away, I'm confused as to why you're upset
I've done a better job than you have since the day we first met.
Sunlight is the bane of my existence
It leaves others to see me unfinished with their curious persistence
Until I'm complete and in the museum I cannot be seen.
My imperfections are still gorgeous but not fit for a queen.

Moon rising is my strength, I crackle and groan coming out of my shell
The gargoyles surround you, the ones you know so well.
You'll meet my demands, swiftly to perfection
Put me in the museum with their most prized collection.
Tirelessly through the day you make and mold
I've done no wrong, your terror is confusing to behold.
Buffing and polishing takes no time, I'm faultless
It's second nature to you, opening night leaves you thoughtless.
Don't worry, I'll stand still. I see the sweat on the back of your neck
Your nervous glances at me and the skylight come into effect.
They're not looking at you, they're looking at me
Craning their necks, I'm the one they're here to see.

Warwick

I'm so tired of breathing your air
Feeling the sharpness of the arrow,
Your sights on me make me more than ever aware
My senses on you narrow.
Blade pointed tip pressed against my neck
Slow controlled breaths
Any sudden movements and this turns into a wreck
Although I have a feeling you'll do it nevertheless.
I can't escape when you have me trapped like an animal within a cage
Keep me pent up and I may just attack
It's like you have me in a circus and I'm performing on stage
Little do they know you have a whip out back.
One wrong move and I'm done for
There is no reasoning or holding you accountable
The smallest mistake and you're war torn,
You're too powerful but I wish your weakness was palpable.
War is like a candle that has a short fuse,
You think it's a candle at first until you light the wick.
You realize it's dynamite, but now you can't choose
There's nothing you can do now except run quick.
I tried to run and leave argument behind,
But someone lit the wick to the war
Now I feel the fury of the forces combined
Yet I have an ace up my sleeve, one you can't ignore.

Helpless Protector

I feel worthless, helpless!
I can't tell you what my point is.
I can't eat, I can't sleep
What's the point if my heart can't even see?
Invisible and broken,
Cold and hurting
I can't do anything, I've lost all control
I'm not an officer, but I'm still on patrol.
Chills roll down my spine like a carpet unrolling,
My shoulders feel the cold phantom hands pressing as if they were
folding.
Withholding and unshowing I must be.
Keep it inside, I'll be fine. Just do it for me.
Hide and seek but I'm hiding
With nobody to seek, but I feel bound and biting.
I'm usually the one to disappear
So where is everyone and why am I the only one here?
Press on my chest and reinforce
I can't breathe. I'm so worried that I'm alone, of course.
I can't lose you too, with love I've put in too much
You're gone now while I've just started to trust.
Come back and please stay
Listen to our love song, I'll press play.
I want to be your hero
It's nigh impossible as I feel like Nero.

Lean on me and rest your heart
The mere thought of you breaks mine when we're apart.
Fight back tears and shaky breath
Lie down in the warmth, try to rest.
Cold emanates from me as ice
Warmth barely reaching me, it'll suffice.
Constantly shaking in adrenaline
How can I not? Please, just let me in.

Powerless to help, I feel lost at sea
I want to protect you, I can! Can't you see?
Except I can't, I'm a million miles away
I can see why you felt the need to escape the fray.
Including me, but what can I do?
I'm someone you see right through.
Not that I'm hiding anything, but I'm glass.
Invisible in fact, at least I'm not like the others: vile and crass.
Some great help they were! Are. You run towards them in childish
glee.
It just happens that you see everyone, but me.
They flaunt it, to be around you they're privileged
Though this is the case they still daily commit sacrilege.
Life changing events don't phase my focus
On you I keep my eyes, no matter how they provoke us.
There may be disaster or frost over the moon
Yet in the end I'm still the one looking at you.

About the Author

R.E. DeLuca is a determined author, who seeks to share the mystics and tall tales that come to mind. With writing as a hobby, they also love enjoying the countryside and exploring the surrounding forests. Their love of nature, animals, poetry, art, and fairy tales can be seen pouring generously through their works.

Read more at redelucawrites.wordpress.com.

www.ingramcontent.com/pod-product-compliance
Lightning Source LLC
Chambersburg PA
CBHW051838130726

47987CB00002B/604